Artists in Their Time

Salvador Dali

Robert Anderson

Franklin Watts
A Division of Scholastic Inc.
New York   Toronto   London   Auckland   Sydney
Mexico City   New Delhi   Hong Kong
Danbury, Connecticut

First published in 2002 by
Franklin Watts
96 Leonard Street,
London EC2A 4XD

First American edition published
in 2002 by Franklin Watts
A Division of Scholastic Inc.
90 Sherman Turnpike
Danbury, CT 06816

Series Editor: Adrian Cole
Series Designer: Mo Choy
Art Director: Jonathan Hair
Picture Researcher: Diana Morris

A CIP catalog record for this title
is available from the Library of Congress.

ISBN 0-531-12231-X (Lib. Bdg.)
ISBN 0-531-16624-4 (Pbk.)

Printed in Hong Kong, China

Acknowledgements

The Advertising Archives: 40. AKG London: 12t. Archive Photos/Hulton Archive : 20tl. Archivio
Iconografico, S.A: Corbis 11 © Salvador Dali, Gala-Salvador Dali Foundation, DACS, London 2002.
Bettmann/Corbis: fr cover bc,19b, 32b. Central Press/Hulton Archive: 25t. Fox Photos/Hulton Archive:
32tl. Daniel Frasnay/AKG London: 20cr, 42. Fundació Gala-Salvador Dalí : 6, 7b, 9t © Salvador Dali, Gala-
Salvador Dali Foundation, DACS, London 2002, 13 © Salvador Dali, Gala-Salvador Dali Foundation,
DACS, London 2002, 33 © Salvador Dali, Gala-Salvador Dali Foundation, DACS, London 2002, 39 ©
Salvador Dali, Gala-Salvador Dali Foundation, DACS, London 2002. © Fundacion Federico Garcia Lorca:
12b, 14t. Galerie Daniel Malingue, Paris: Bridgeman 18t © ADAGP,Paris and DACS, London 2002. Robert
Harding PL: 7t, 8. Charles Hewitt/Picture Post/Hulton Archive: 22bl. Hulton Archive: fr cover br,18b, 24b,
30tl, 34, 36b. Courtesy of Kobal Collection: 16tl, 17, 35b. Kunsthalle, Hamburg: Bridgeman 10 © DACS
2002. Louvre, Paris: Bridgeman 14b, Giraudon/Bridgeman 30c. Courtesy Lee Miller Archives: 28t. Museum
of Modern Art, New York: Artothek fr cover c & 21 © Salvador Dali, Gala-Salvador Dali Foundation,
DACS, London 2002, 23 © Salvador Dali, Gala-Salvador Dali Foundation, DACS, London 2002. Musée
National d'Art Moderne, Paris: Lauros-Giraudon/Bridgeman 35t © ARS, NY and DACS, London, 2002.
Musée d'Orsay, Paris: Bridgeman 22t. Philadelphia Museum of Art: Corbis 28b. Prado, Madrid:
Giraudon/Bridgeman 26b. Private Collection: Index/Bridgeman 15 © Salvador Dali, Gala-Salvador Dali
Foundation, DACS, London 2002 : Lauros-Giraudon/Bridgeman 24t © ADAGP, Paris and DACS, London
2002. Rex Features: 41t. Ewa Rudling/Sipa Press/Rex Features: 41b. St Mungo Museum of Religious Art,
Glasgow: Artothek 37 © Glasgow Museums: The St Mungo Museum of Religious Life & Art. Sipa
Press/Rex Features: 36b, 38. Tate Picture Library: 26t detail © Salvador Dali, Gala-Salvador Dali
Foundation, DACS, London 2002, 27 © Salvador Dali, Gala-Salvador Dali Foundation, DACS, London
2002, 29 © Salvador Dali, Gala-Salvador Dali Foundation, DACS, London 2002, 31 © Salvador Dali, Gala-
Salvador Dali Foundation, DACS, London 2002. Topical Press Agency/Hulton Archive: 16tr.

Whilst every attempt has been made to clear copyright
should there be any inadvertent omission please apply
in the first instance to the publisher regarding rectification.

Contents

Who Was Salvador Dali?

Salvador Dali was born Salvador Felipe Jacinto Dali Domènech on May 11, 1904, in Figueres, a town situated in a region of northeast Spain called Catalonia.

Dali's father, also named Salvador, was an important and respected person in Figueres. He had many friends in the town, some of whom were writers or painters. Dali's mother, Felipa, was a devout Roman Catholic. She was loving and very warmhearted. Dali later described her as the "honey of the family."

"At the age of six I wanted to be a cook. At seven I wanted to be Napoleon. And my ambition has been growing steadily ever since."

Salvador Dali

▲ Salvador Dali, at age five, in a park in Barcelona. As a boy, Dali was pampered and spoiled. His older brother died while still a baby, less than a year before Dali's birth.

DAYDREAMER

The young Salvador and his younger sister, Ana Mariá, spent most of their childhood in and around the comfortable family apartment in the bustling center of town. Between the ages of six and twelve, Salvador went to a Roman Catholic primary school run by French priests. He was very intelligent, although he found it difficult to concentrate on his work during lessons. He often found himself daydreaming in the classroom. Sometimes he doodled all over his school books. At other times, he stared at the stains on the classroom ceiling made by the leaky roof, and imagined they were all sorts of wonderful things.

NATURAL INSPIRATION

On weekends and during long, hot, summer vacations, the Dali family went to the seaside village of Cadaqués. There they had a house surrounded by beautiful gardens, fields, and orange groves. Salvador and Ana Mariá spent their days exploring the rock pools and beaches, or watching their father's friends painting the breathtaking views across the Mediterranean Sea. The Dalis' house was always full of aunts, uncles, and cousins, as well as many other guests. Despite this ideal life, Dali remembered his childhood as sometimes troubled and unhappy.

▲ The picturesque fishing village of Cadaqués remained Dali's favorite place throughout his life. Its beaches and cliffs are in many of his paintings.

▲ The Dali family at Cadaqués around 1910. Left to right is Dali's aunt Mariá Teresa, his mother and father, Salvador himself, his aunt Catalina, his sister, Ana Mariá, and his grandmother Ana.

MEMORIES AND MYTHS

In 1942, Dali published his autobiography, or life story, which he called *The Secret Life of Salvador Dali*. In it, Dali made up many stories about his childhood. For instance, he wrote that his older brother had died at age seven and that his parents always loved his brother more than him. In reality, his brother died when he was still a baby, less than a year before Dali was born. Dali saw nothing wrong with making up stories. He claimed that they told an "emotional" truth that went far deeper than simple facts.

An Artist From Catalonia

▲ One of the most astonishing sights that Dali saw in Barcelona was the church of the Sagrada Familia designed by Antonio Gaudí. The church's "melting" shapes helped inspire Dali's Surrealist masterpieces.

Dali's father often took him to Barcelona, the Catalan capital. At the time, the city was flourishing, and there were new buildings and parks to see. Many of the buildings were designed by the famous architect Antonio Gaudí (1852-1926). His most famous building is the Sagrada Familia, or Holy Family, a church so extravagant that it is still under construction.

Barcelona had many busy cafés. One of the most popular was the els Quatre Gats. Painters and writers gathered there to discuss the latest ideas from Paris. At the time, Paris was at the forefront of new developments in art. Many Spanish artists, including Pablo Picasso (1881-1971), lived and worked there.

VIOLENCE AND TRAGEDY

In spite of its prosperity, Barcelona was sometimes rocked by unrest and violence. The city's many factory workers were usually poorly paid and treated badly. Some supported the socialist and communist ideas of Karl Marx (1818-83). Others supported anarchism, which is the belief that people should be able to live their lives free of church or government laws.

TIMELINE ▶

May 11, 1904	1907	1908	1909	1914	1914-18	1917
Salvador Dali Domènech is born in Figueres, Catalonia, Spain.	The Spanish artist Pablo Picasso paints his first Cubist pictures in Paris.	Dali's sister, Ana Mariá, is born.	The "Tragic Week": workers strike in Barcelona.	Gaudí's Güell Park opens.	World War I; Spain does not take part.	Dali holds an exhibition of his paintings in the family apartment.

▲ *Portrait of My Father*, 1920. Dali painted this portrait at age sixteen. The shimmering colors and lively brushstrokes clearly show the influence of a group of French artists known as the Impressionists.

In 1909, many Barcelona workers rose up against the government and burned down churches and schools. The army stopped the uprising, and 116 people died. Catalans still remember this terrible event as the "Tragic Week."

YOUTHFUL PROMISE

Anarchist and socialist ideas were popular among Dali's classmates, but Dali chose to concentrate on what he loved best, drawing and painting. He started to draw and paint as a very young boy. His parents encouraged him and even gave him his own studio. At the age of thirteen, Dali won a prize for his drawing, and his proud father threw a party to celebrate. Dali's early paintings included seaside views of sailing boats, whitewashed houses, and green olive groves. He also made portraits of his father, whom he often showed wearing a suit and a heavy, gold watch and chain. Even as a teenager, Dali experimented with the bold new styles from Paris.

CATALONIA

Until the 18th century, Catalonia was an independent country, separate from Spain. To this day, Catalonia's people – the Catalans – remain very proud of their local traditions and customs, including their own language, Catalan. Dali's father was a strong supporter of Catalan culture. Catalan was spoken in the family home, although Dali was taught to speak Spanish and French as well. Throughout his life Dali was proud of his homeland and he often wore a *barretina* (see page 36), a traditional Catalan soft hat.

  Catalonia's landscape is comprised of a great, rugged plain and a long coastline of rocky beaches that are washed by the warm Mediterranean Sea. Catalonia's capital, the port of Barcelona, is on the coast. Dali was born in the town of Figueres, which lies in the far north of Catalonia, about 60 miles (97 km) northeast of Barcelona. This small, prosperous town is nestled at the foot of the Pyrenees Mountains, not very far from Spain's border with France.

▲ Catalonia lies in the northeast corner of Spain. The surrounding mountains and sea helped keep the region apart from the rest of the country and gave it a strong, separate identity.

9

Studying in Madrid

In 1922, Dali, now age seventeen, went to the Spanish capital, Madrid, to study at the San Fernando Academy of Fine Art. Dali quickly became unhappy with the teaching given by the academy's professors. He preferred to wander around Madrid's huge art museum, the Prado. There he admired the works of the great Spanish painters, such as Diego Velázquez (1599-1660) and Francisco de Goya (1746-1828). He also kept close contact with the latest developments in modern art.

◄ *Melancholy: The Street*, **Giorgio de Chirico, 1924.** In this painting, de Chirico uses a traditional, realistic style to create a disturbing image of a small girl running down a deeply shadowed street.

AN ECCENTRIC STUDENT

In Madrid, Dali lived in a university residence. There he met a group of radical young writers and painters, including Federico Garcia Lorca (1898-1936) and Luis Buñuel (1900-83). The students led a wild life in Madrid's cafés and night clubs. Dali became known as an eccentric. One of his favorite tricks was to let a banknote dissolve in his beverage before he drank it.

NEW KINDS OF ART

During and after World War I (1914-18), many European painters grew tired of the endless experiments of the previous decades and began to paint in more traditional ways. Artists such as Italian painter Giorgio de Chirico (1888-1978) rejected the bold colors used by the Expressionists and the shattered shapes of the Cubists. Instead, they painted in a straightforward fashion, using sober colors and conventional techniques such as perspective. However, they often put these old styles of painting to new uses by creating startling or even disturbing images. Dali found this approach very exciting.

TIMELINE ▶

1917	February 1921	October 1921	1922	October 1922	1923
Revolution in Russia brings about the world's first communist government.	Dali's mother dies.	Dali goes to Madrid to study at the San Fernando Academy of Fine Arts.	The Surrealist group forms in Paris, led by André Breton.	Benito Mussolini becomes Fascist dictator of Italy.	Sigmund Freud's *The Interpretation of Dreams* is published in Spanish.

Portrait of Luis Buñuel, 1924

oil on canvas, 26 x 23 in (68.5 x 58.5 cm), Museo Nacional Central de Arte Reina Sofia, Madrid, Spain

Luis Buñuel was one of Dali's closest friends at his student residence in Madrid and later became a famous Surrealist filmmaker. In his portrait, Dali shows his friend standing in a strange, wintery landscape and uses only a few gloomy colors and shades – brown, grey, black, and white.

Close Friends

▲ Picasso in his studio in 1929.

DALI AND PICASSO

For Dali, Pablo Picasso was the greatest living painter. At the beginning of the 20th century, Picasso helped pioneer a revolutionary new art known as Cubism. A Cubist painting shows several views of a subject at once. During the 1920s, Dali produced his own Cubist pictures, including *Pierrot Playing the Guitar*.

Picasso saw and praised Dali's exhibition at the Dalmau. In 1926, Dali visited Paris for the first time. The moment he arrived, Dali went to visit Picasso at his studio. On meeting him, Dali declared, "I have visited you before going to the Louvre." The Louvre is one of the world's greatest art museums.

In 1923, a Spanish general named Miguel Primo de Rivera set up a dictatorship in Spain. Dali's father opposed the regime, and the government took revenge by sending his son to prison for thirty-five days. The young Dali did not seem to mind prison very much and spent his time drawing.

POETRY AND PAINTING

Dali's closest friend during the 1920s was the poet Federico Garcia Lorca. Lorca came from the hot, sunny region of Andalucía, in the far south of Spain. His poetry is full of passion and dreamlike images. The two friends admired each other's work deeply, and each felt that their art evolved as a result of their friendship. They grew so close that Dali thought of himself and Lorca almost as a single person, just as he showed in *Pierrot Playing the Guitar*.

◀ Dali (left) and Lorca (right) in Cadaqués. After his first visit there, Lorca wrote a poem in praise of Dali.

"May stars like falconless fists shine on you, while your painting and your life break into flower."

Federico Garcia Lorca, from his Ode to Salvador Dali

In 1925, Barcelona's most important art gallery, Dalmau, gave Dali his first exhibition. The critics wrote favorably about the new, young artist, and Dali sold many paintings. He only sent Lorca his bad reviews, saying "the others aren't of interest because they are so enthusiatic."

TIMELINE ▶

September 1923	October 1923	May 1924	October 1924	March 1925	November 1925	April 1926
Miguel Primo de Rivera sets up a dictatorship in Spain.	The San Fernando Academy suspends Dali.	Dali serves a one-month prison sentence.	Breton launches the first *Surrealist Manifesto* in Paris.	Lorca goes with Dali to Cadaqués. Close friendship develops.	The Dalmau Gallery holds Dali's first solo exhibition.	Dali makes his first trip to Paris and visits Picasso and Joan Miró.

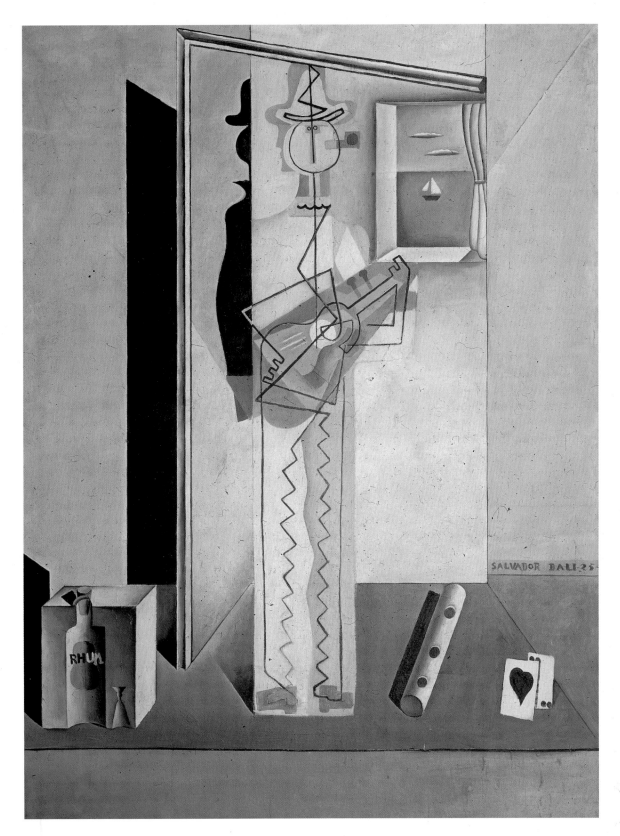

Pierrot Playing the Guitar, 1925

oil on canvas, 78 x 58 $^2/_3$ in (198 x 149 cm), Museo Nacional Central de Arte Reina Sofia, Madrid, Spain

Pierrot was a clownlike character from French pantomimes and is featured in several of Picasso's paintings. In this picture of Pierrot, Dali mixed up his own features with those of his friend Lorca. On the floor is a bottle, a flute, and some playing cards. The ace of hearts suggests the tender friendship that united the two men.

Painting From Life

Dali did not concentrate on one style of art in his early years. In developing his art, he imitated and experimented with many different styles and was open to influences from avant-garde painters and Old Masters of the past.

PAST MASTERS

Throughout his life, Dali admired the great artists of the past. One of his favorite pictures was *The Lacemaker* by the Dutch artist Jan Vermeer (1632-75). This tiny painting shows a girl working intently on a delicate piece of lace. Lacemaking requires skill and patience and was traditionally done by women at home. Vermeer's beautiful painting inspired Dali to paint his own sister at work on a piece of lace.

A MODEL SISTER

Dali spent his vacations from the Madrid academy at home at Figueres or at the seaside in Cadaqués. His paintings of this time often showed his sister looking out across Figueres harbor or quietly working. He also painted still lifes, or pictures of everyday objects, such as fruit and bread, and knives and bottles.

▲ **Dali with Ana Mariá in Cadaqués, 1925.**

EXPELLED

In October of 1926, Dali was expelled from the San Fernando Academy shortly before graduating. He refused to finish his final examinations. His excuse was that he knew more than his examiner. Perhaps he was right, he already had a growing reputation and his work had attracted the attention of not only Picasso but the Catalan artist Joan Miró (1893-1983). However, Dali's extraordinary self-confidence and boastfulness were an important part of his personality.

◀ *The Lacemaker*, **Jan Vermeer, 1669-70.**
Vermeer's painting is less than 10 inches (25 cm) high. Its intricate detail matches the painstaking work of the servant girl.

TIMELINE ▶

October 1926	January 1927	February 1927	June 1927	September 1927
Dali is expelled from the San Fernando Academy.	Dali has his second one-man show. Includes *Woman Sewing at a Window in Figueres.*	Dali begins a 9 month military service based in Figueres.	Lorca's play *Mariana Pineda* opens in Barcelona, Dali designs set and costumes.	The Catalan Surrealist artist Joan Miró visits Dali and later writes to encourage him to move to Paris.

Woman at the Window Sewing in Figueres, 1926

oil on canvas, 9 7/16 x 9 5/16 in (24 x 25 cm), Private Collection

Ana Mariá sits on a balcony overlooking Figueres's main square. In the background are the blue Pyrenees Mountains. The budding trees tell us it is the beginning of spring. Like Vermeer, Dali shows us just what it feels like to be deeply absorbed in a task – whether it is lacemaking or painting.

"Those who do not want to imitate anything produce nothing."

Salvador Dali

Making a Surrealist Movie

▲ A poster for *Battleship Potemkin*, a film directed by Sergei Eisenstein.

MONTAGE

In their movie, Dali and Buñuel used a new technique called montage to startle the audience. In filmmaking, montage means a rapid succession of different images. The pioneer of montage was Russian filmmaker Sergei Eisenstein (1898–1948). Earlier filmmakers had simply let the camera run, so watching a film was like watching a play at a theater. In the 1920s, Eisenstein developed a way of editing together different shots to make his films more gripping by quickly cutting from one viewpoint to another.

In the late 1920s, Dali became increasingly attracted to the art of the Surrealists. He began experimenting with their strange, dreamlike images. The Catalan Surrealist Joan Miró encouraged Dali to go to Paris. When Dali made it to Paris, Miró told him that he would find success.

▲ During the 1920s and 30s, Paris was the artistic capital of the world.

INSPIRED BY DREAMS

In early 1929, Dali began working on a Surrealist movie with his old college friend Luis Buñuel. The movie was inspired by their dreams. Buñuel's dream was of a cloud slicing the moon in half, while Dali's was of a hand swarming with ants. In April, Dali went to Paris to shoot the movie with Buñuel. The movie was called *Un chien andalou*, or *An Andalusian Dog*.

Un chien andalou was unlike any other movie made before and it attracted a great deal of attention. The movie ran for eight months at a theater in Paris. It is only seventeen minutes long, and is made up of a series of dreamlike images, which includes a hand crawling with ants and a dead donkey lying over a grand piano.

TIMELINE ▶

March 1928	April 1929	Summer 1929	October 1929	November 1929
Dali publishes the *Yellow Manifesto* denouncing Catalan art.	Dali goes to Paris to make the film *Un chien andalou* with Luis Buñuel.	Dali begins affair with Gala Éluard, wife of Surrealist poet Paul Éluard (1895–1952). Dali's father bans him from the family home.	*Un chien andalou* opens to the public in Paris. The Wall Street Crash: economic depression hits the United States and Europe.	Dali has his first exhibition in Paris.

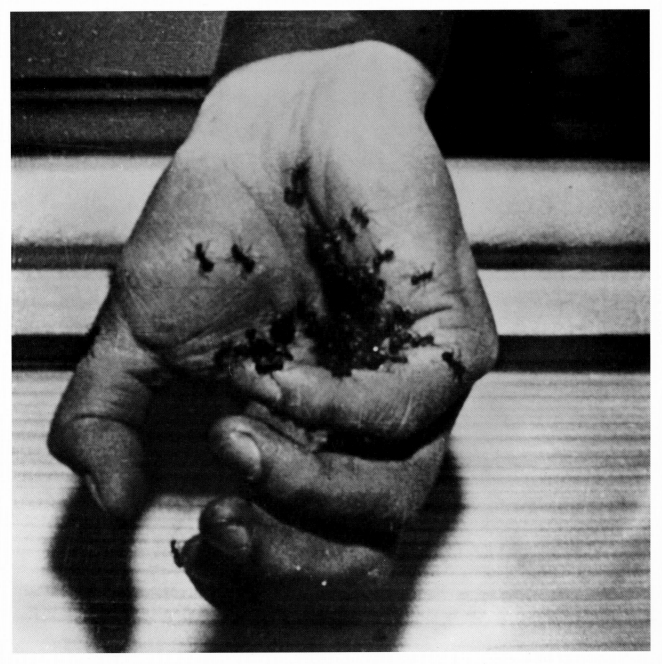

Still from *Un chien andalou*, 1929

This is just one of many strange and unnerving images in Dali and Buñuel's movie. Another scene includes shots of a cork, a melon, two Roman Catholic priests, and two grand pianos, on each of which is a dead donkey. Dali included ants in many of his paintings. For Dali they were a symbol of death and decay. As a child, he had rescued a bat but later found it dead and swarming with ants.

"Why ... did a black hole appear in the middle of my palm, filled with a swarming anthill that I try to scoop out with a spoon?"

Salvador Dali

Surrealism

*U*n *chien andalou* firmly established Dali at the center of the Surrealist movement. The Surrealists liked the movie because it used many of their ideas.

INTERPRETING DREAMS

The Surrealists explored the world of dreams. They were not the first artists to do this, but they were the first to take much of their inspiration from the Austrian thinker Sigmund Freud (1856-1939). In his book *The Interpretation of Dreams* (1900), Freud showed how a psychiatrist could help people solve their problems by analyzing, or interpreting, their dreams. Freud believed dreams could reveal the unconscious mind.

▲ *Dialogue of Insects*, Joan Miró, 1924-25.
André Breton called Miró "the most surrealist of all." This painting is typical of Miró's work in the 1920s, full of joyous colors and childlike imagination.

BETTER THAN REAL

"Surreal" was a made-up word, meaning "more than real" or "better than real." The leader of the group was the French poet André Breton (1896-1966). In 1924, Breton organized the publication of the first *Surrealist Manifesto*, which outlined the group's ideas. The first exhibition of Surrealist paintings took place in Paris in 1925, and included works by the German Max Ernst (1891-1976) and Joan Miró. Soon many other artists in Europe and the United States used the Surrealists' ideas. Dali belonged to this second, younger generation. The older Surrealists, including Breton, quickly recognized Dali's importance.

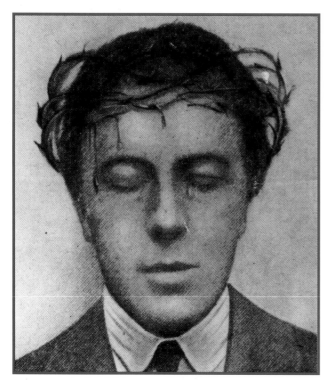

◄ André Breton as he was pictured in the first *Surrealist Manifesto* in 1924.

UNCOMFORTABLE ART

The Surrealists disliked much of the art of their time because they felt it was too cosy and comfortable. They particularly despised the work of the French painter Henri Matisse (1869-1954). Matisse once declared that a good painting should be just as soothing as "a good armchair." By contrast, the Surrealists wanted to shock and unsettle the people who looked at their pictures, forcing them to think rather than just look.

One way the Surrealists did this was to put objects together in unusual combinations – for example placing a donkey on a piano, as Dali and Buñuel did in *Un chien andalou*. Sometimes the Surrealists did this by using a collage, which combined photographs and words cut out of newspapers and magazines. Another Surrealist technique was frottage. This involved making rubbings of an object and then using the shapes and textures produced as a starting point for a drawing or painting.

The people who saw the Surrealist pictures at the time were often shocked or surprised. Today, we see "surreal" images everywhere. They are on television shows and in advertisements everyday. Since we see these images everyday they do not shock us. The original Surrealist pictures, however, can still be very disturbing.

> *"The art of Dali [is] the most hallucinatory known."*
>
> André Breton

▼ A Surrealist exhibition in Paris in 1938. The Surrealists loved to shock people. Here they have turned a gallery into a bedroom and a jungle.

To Confuse and Disturb

Dali was now an important member of the Surrealist group. He was even chosen to design the opening image of the *Second Surrealist Manifesto* published in 1930. In that year, Dali and Gala Éluard went to live in a cottage at Port Lligat, just outside of Cadaqués. Here Dali painted some of his most famous paintings, including *The Persistence of Memory*.

▲ Albert Einstein, c.1925. His ideas about time and space revolutionized the way people look at the world.

DALI AND EINSTEIN

Dali was fascinated by the ideas of the scientist Albert Einstein (1879–1955). Einstein's theories about the nature of time and space changed the way people looked at the world. Before Einstein, people thought of the world as solid and constant. Einstein, however, suggested that everything was in flux. Even time, for instance, does not flow constantly but slows down or speeds up according to circumstances. Einstein's idea is known as the "Theory of Relativity."

◀ Dali and Gala's house at Port Lligat. Over the years, the couple transformed a fisherman's cottage into a large and beautiful home with a studio. Today the house is a museum devoted to Dali and his work.

DOUBLE TAKE

At this time, Dali was developing his own ideas about Surrealism and published them in a book called *The Visible Woman* (1930). He felt that Surrealist artists should depict a kind of madness or fever in which a thing could look like one thing at one moment and like another the next. Many of Dali's paintings used these "double" images to confuse and disturb people looking at them. For example, at the center of *The Persistence of Memory* a watch flops over what looks like a strange, pale-colored rock. However, if we look at it more closely, the rock looks like a person curled up on the sand.

TIMELINE ▶

January 1930	April 1930	Summer 1930	October 1930	December 1930	1931
De Rivera's rule in Spain ends, partly because of the economic depression.	*The Second Surrealist Manifesto* is published. Dali designs its opening image.	Dali and Gala buy and begin to restore a fisherman's cottage at Port Lligat, Cadaqués.	*L'Âge d'or*, a new Dali-Buñuel movie, opens in Paris. It is later banned after newspaper protests.	*The Visible Woman* is published.	Spain is declared a republic.

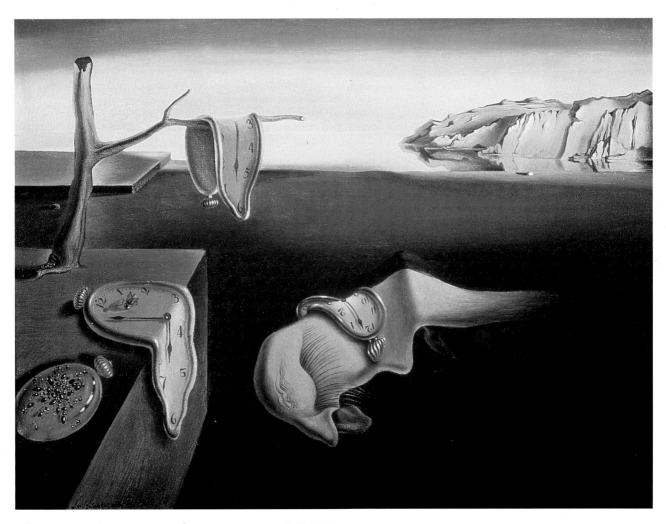

The Persistence of Memory, 1931

oil on canvas, 9 1/2 x 13 in (24 x 33 cm), The Museum of Modern Art, New York, New York

Dali called his paintings "hand-painted dream photographs." By this, he meant that the things he painted often look very real – like photographs – but at the same time are impossible or improbable – like dreams. Here he uses his technique to show watches melting on a hot beach. One watch hangs limply from a dead tree; another attracts a swarm of ants (see page 17). All the watches tell different times. The painting seems to portray just the kind of unstable, uncertain world Einstein proposed in his "Theory of Relativity."

"It will be possible to systematize confusion and contribute to the total discrediting of the world of reality."

Salvador Dali on using double imagery, The Visible Woman

Love and Marriage

In 1934, Dali finally married Gala. She had been his muse and great love ever since they had met in 1929. At the time, Gala was already married to the Surrealist poet Paul Éluard (1895-1952). Dali's father was so angered by Dali and Gala's relationship that he threw Dali out of the family home. In protest, Dali shaved off his hair.

Dali adored Gala. She had helped him recover from a deep depression that he had suffered from before they met, and he often used her as a model. They spent most of their time happily at Port Lligat.

Dali's success continued. Shortly after his marriage, he had his first London exhibition. A little later the couple traveled to New York, where they received a lot of flattering attention.

▲ *The Angelus*, Jean-François Millet, **1857-59.** The Angelus is a Christian prayer said at morning, noon, and evening.

▲ Dali poses Gala for one of his paintings at Port Lligat. He thought the shape of her back and hips was that of the perfect female.

THE ANGELUS OF GALA

Dali painted this portrait of Gala a few years after they first met. He shows her from both the front and back, just as if she were looking in a mirror. However, there is no mirror to be seen. There are also some odd differences between the two Galas. While one of them is sitting on a box, the other is perched on a wheelbarrow.

In the background there is a picture of two farm workers praying in a field at dusk. Dali based the picture on a popular painting called *The Angelus* by the 19th-century French artist Jean-François Millet (1814-75). A copy of the painting had hung in Dali's first school and haunted Dali throughout his life.

TIMELINE ▶

January 1933	November 1933	1934	January 1934	October 1934	November 1934
Nazi party comes to power in Germany, under leader Adolf Hitler.	Dali has his first solo exhibition in the United States at the Julien Levy Gallery, New York.	Dali quarrels with André Breton. Begins to move away from the Surrealist group.	Dali marries Gala.	Dali has his first solo exhibition in Britain, at the Zwemmer Gallery, London.	Dali and Gala visit New York for the first time.

The Angelus of Gala, 1935

oil on panel, 12 3/4 x 10 1/2 in (32 x 27 cm) Museum of Modern Art, New York, New York

Dali leaves us unsure whether it is Gala who is praying or whether the painting is itself a kind of prayer to his wife. Whatever we decide, the picture shows Dali's deep devotion to Gala. As in many of his pictures, Dali painted this portrait in a painstaking way, paying a lot of attention to detail. Gala's beautiful embroidered jacket, for example, could almost be real.

The Spanish Civil War

While Dali was enjoying his international success, the situation in Spain was less happy. From 1936 to 1939, a bloody civil war raged in Spain. The Spanish Civil War was fought between those who believed that Spain should be a monarchy – that is, ruled by a king – and those who thought it should be a republic led by an elected president. Many republicans were ordinary workers or the supporters of left-wing parties such as the socialists and communists. The monarchists, by contrast, were often landowners and business people, or members of the army or the Roman Catholic Church.

A NEW REPUBLIC

For hundreds of years, Spain had been a monarchy. However, in 1931, the Spanish people voted for their country to become a republic. The new government carried out wide-ranging reforms and gave regions such as Catalonia more independence.

▲ *Aidez l'Espagne*, **Joan Miró, 1937.**
Joan Miró was a passionate supporter of the Republicans. This poster calls on the French to "Help Spain" and fight against Franco.

AN END TO REFORMS

Many Spanish people came to believe that the reforms were too extreme. In 1933, a new government came to power and brought an end to the reforms. In some parts of Spain, workers rebelled against the government. In Barcelona, for example, workers declared Catalonia an independent republic. Government soldiers brutally ended the revolts, killing more than a thousand people.

◄ The Nationalist leader, General Franco, was ruthless in his determination to overthrow the elected Republican government.

▲ Civilians defend a makeshift barricade in Barcelona, 1937. Most people in Barcelona supported the Republican cause.

In 1936, the Spanish president called for another election. This time, the left-wing republican parties won by a small number of votes. Right after the election a monarchist rebellion broke out. The rebels, led by General Francisco Franco (1892-1975), soon gained control of about a third of Spain. The rebels were known as Nationalists. The forces who defended the republic were called Loyalists or Republicans.

FOREIGN INTERVENTION
Neither side was strong enough to win the war quickly, and sought help from abroad. Hitler's Nazi Germany and Mussolini's Fascist Italy, sent tanks, planes, and soldiers to help the Nationalists. The communist Soviet Union sent military aid to the Republicans. In addition, thousands of volunteers came from all over the world to help the Republican cause.

Altogether more than 500,000 Spaniards died as a result of the war. Many of these were civilians, or non-soldiers, who were killed when their towns and cities were bombed or died due to lack of food. Eventually, in March of 1939, the Nationalists defeated the Republicans and General Franco established a dictatorship. He was to remain in power for over thirty-five years.

TAKING SIDES
During the Spanish Civil War, most Spanish artists, including Pablo Picasso and Joan Miró, supported the Republicans. In 1937, Picasso produced a huge painting to commemorate the Spanish town of Guernica, which had been bombed by German planes. The Surrealists also supported the Republicans. Dali refused to support either side, even after the Nationalists executed his friend Fredrico García Lorca in 1936.

The Horror of War

Although Dali did not take sides in the Spanish Civil War, he was horrified by the destruction it caused. He painted *Autumn Cannibalism* soon after the outbreak of the war. In this famous painting, two monstrous human beings dine off of each other's bodies. The first person scoops out a spoonful of the second person's flesh, while the second person slices into the first person's skin.

A SPANISH TRADITION

Dali was not the first Spanish artist to try to convey the horror of war. In the early 19th century, the Spanish artist Francisco Goya was moved to paint by another period of war in Spain's history and produced many pictures on the subject. In *The Colossus* (below), Goya showed a fierce giant spreading fear and panic among hundreds of people. Many experts think that Goya's "colossus," or giant figure, is a symbol of war. In another picture, he depicted the giant Roman God, Saturn eating his own child. Like Dali, he uses cannibalism to show his disgust of war.

▲ The brushstrokes in this close-up of *Autumn Cannibalism* are invisible.

IN DETAIL

Dali created his paintings with a lot of care. Many artists at this time painted very freely, using big, bold brushstrokes that are visible in their paintings. By contrast, Dali painted so that we are unable to see a single brushstroke, making his pictures appear smooth and glossy. This way of painting was sometimes called "academic" and was very popular in the 19th century.

Dali used the academic style to make the strangest things seem real. In the detail of *Autumn Cannibalism* above, it is hard not to shudder as you watch the shiny, metal knife slice into the soft, caramel-colored flesh.

▲ *The Colossus*, **Francisco Goya, c. 1810.** Many artists have tried to show the pointless destruction caused by war. Goya painted this after the troops of the French emperor Napoleon invaded Spain in 1809.

Autumn Cannibalism, 1936

oil on canvas, 25 5/8 x 25 5/8 in (65 x 65 cm), Tate Modern, London, England

This gruesome painting uses mostly gloomy colors – chocolate browns and milky greys. Even the sky is grey and empty, except for a looming storm cloud. Drawers, such as the one bottom right, featured in many of Dali's pictures about this time – he saw them both as a symbol of the hidden unconscious and also as a source of bad smells, in this case the smell of war.

"From all parts of martyred Spain rose a smell ... of burned curates' fat and of quartered spiritual flesh that mingled with the smell of ... death."

Salvador Dali

Star of the Show

DALI AND DESIGN

From the 1930s, Dali spent a lot of his time designing Surrealist objects as well as painting. Some critics even think that Dali was a better designer than painter. Dali was interested in fashion and designed extravagant jewelery and clothes. He worked closely with Italian designer Elsa Schiaparelli (1890-1973). They created a women's suit with pockets that looked like drawers, as well as a dress with a lobster, parsley, and mayonnaise pattern.

▶ Dali and Elsa Schiaparelli's lobster dress.

▲ Dali in his diving suit with other Surrealist painters and writers in London in 1936.

Despite the civil war, Dali continued to travel and his international reputation reached new heights. In 1936, there was an exhibition of Surrealist art in London. Dali was the star of the show. He attracted a lot of attention from the press, especially when he gave a lecture at the gallery while wearing a diving suit. Some Surrealist artists, especially Breton, criticized Dali for seeking fame. Breton was a communist, and he also accused Dali of supporting right-wing extremists such as the German dictator, Adolf Hitler.

SURREALIST FURNITURE

At this time, Dali became friends with an English millionaire named Edward James. From 1936 to 1939, James gave Dali a monthly income in return for all of his paintings and drawings. Dali also created Surrealist pieces of furniture for James, including a pink sofa in the shape of lips, a telephone with a lobster instead of a receiver, and a chair with hands.

TIMELINE ▶

June 1936	July 1936	August 1936	December 1936	December 1936
The International Surrealist Exhibition opens in London. Dali lectures at it dressed in a diving suit.	The Spanish Civil War begins.	Lorca is killed by Nationalists.	Dali signs a contract with Edward James ensuring a monthly income for next 3 years.	Dali appears on the front cover of the U.S. magazine *Time*.

Lobster Telephone, 1936
telephone with painted plaster lobster, 6 x 11 13/16 x 6 11/16 in (15 x 30 x 17 cm), Tate Modern, London, England
Imagine answering a telephone like this! Dali's sense of the absurd and ridiculous is apparent in "Surrealist" objects like this one.

"It is not necessary for the public to know whether I am joking or whether I am serious, just as it is not necessary for me to know it myself."

Salvador Dali

Painting the Unconscious Mind

In 1938, Dali went to visit the famous thinker Sigmund Freud in London and drew several pictures of him. He also showed him his painting *The Metamorphosis of Narcissus*.

ROMAN MYTH

The ancient Roman writer Ovid told a story about a handsome young man named Narcissus. Looking into a pool, Narcissus fell so in love with his own reflection that he was unable to move. Eventually, he died and the gods changed him into a spring flower – the narcissus.

DALI AND FREUD

Freud's ideas about the human personality were a powerful influence on Dali's work and the Surrealists as a whole (see page 18). Freud described a condition in which a person becomes so obsessed with himself that he is unable to love anyone else. Freud called this condition narcissism, after the legendary Narcissus. Freud often used characters in ancient myth to describe particular psychological types – another example is the "Oedipus complex," a condition where a man is obsessed with his mother. Oedipus was a character from ancient Greek myth who mistakenly married his mother.

▲ *Echo and Narcissus*, **Nicolas Poussin, 1627-28.** Many artists have painted the story of Narcissus. In this version by the 17th-century French painter Poussin, Narcissus lies dead as narcissus flowers sprout from his head.

In Dali's painting, we can see Narcissus both before and after his metamorphosis, or change. On the left, Narcissus kneels over a pool. On the right, both his body and reflection have turned to stone. His head has become an egg, out of which bursts a white flower. There is another Narcissus in the painting, can you find it?

TIMELINE ▶

January 1937	June 1937	July 1937	January 1938	March 1938	July 1938
Dali travels to Hollywood and meets the Marx brothers.	Picasso shows *Guernica*, his famous anti-war picture.	Dali paints *The Metamorphosis of Narcissus* and writes a poem of the same name.	International Surrealists Exhibition opens in Paris. Dali takes part in it.	Hitler makes Austria part of Germany. Breton and Surrealists condemn Dali's comments on Hitler.	Dali meets Freud in London.

The Metamorphosis of Narcissus, 1937

oil on canvas, 20 x 31 in (51 x 78 cm), Tate Modern, London, England

In his painting, Dali shows how the self-love of narcissism can lead to death and decay. However, he also suggests that narcissism is not all negative, that it may create beautiful things, such as the springtime flower. The story of Narcissus fascinated Dali. He even wrote a long poem about it at the same time he was working on this painting.

"They ... scent out the countless narcissistic smells that waft out of all our drawers."

Salvador Dali on Freud's theories

The Power of Hitler

▲ Hitler stands next to Chamberlain (second from right) after signing the Munich Pact in September of 1938.

In 1938, the German dictator, Adolf Hitler, sent troops into the neighboring country of Austria. He had never tried to hide the fact that he wanted to build a mighty German empire and aggressively pursued his goal. Other European countries tried to keep the peace (see panel), and let Hitler take part of Czechoslovakia (the modern Czech Republic and Slovakia), too.

Dali was fascinated by Hitler's power and charisma, although he did not always admire his beliefs. Many of the other Surrealists were communists and opposed Hitler wholeheartedly. They accused Dali of supporting Hitler, and eventually expelled him from the group.

LOOMING WAR

In 1938, Britain's prime minister, Neville Chamberlain (1869-1940), went to Munich to meet Hitler, hoping to avoid war. Britain's policy was known as "Appeasement." At the meeting, Hitler and Chamberlain agreed that Germany could take over the Sudetenland, which was part of Czechoslovakia. Chamberlain returned to Britain claiming he brought "peace in our time." Dali painted *The Enigma of Hitler* soon after this event, unconvinced by the agreement. History proved him right. By March of 1939, Hitler's armies had taken over all of Czechoslovakia.

EUROPE AT WAR

In September of 1939, German troops invaded Poland, and Britain declared war on Germany. The Second World War had begun. At the time, Dali and Gala were in Paris. At first, they moved to southwest France, far away from any possible fighting. However in 1940, Germany invaded and occupied France. Dali and Gala, along with many other writers and artists, decided to leave for the safe haven of the United States.

▲ Dali stands on deck as his ship arrives in New York, 1936. During this trip, he received a lot of press attention. At the end of the year, he even appeared on the cover of the popular *Time* magazine. When Dali returned to the city in 1940, he was already a celebrity there.

TIMELINE ▶

September 1938	Early 1939	September 1939	June 1940	August 1940	November 1941	December 1941	October 1942
Chamberlain meets Hitler in Munich.	Surrealist group expels Dali. Spanish Civil War ends.	World War II begins. Spain remains neutral.	Germany occupies France.	Dali and Gala escape to the United States.	Dali and Miró joint exhibition at the Museum of Modern Art, New York.	The United States enters war after Japan bombs Pearl Harbor.	Dali publishes his autobiography, *The Secret Life of Salvador Dali.*

The Enigma of Hitler, 1939

oil on canvas, 20 ⅙ x 31 ¼ in (51.2 x 79.3 cm), Museo Nacional Central de Arte Reina Sofia, Madrid, Spain

The Enigma of Hitler is full of gloom and the threat of war. A photograph of Hitler, torn out of a newspaper, lies on a plate. One end of a giant black telephone receiver is turning into a lobster claw, showing how war is breaking out, despite all the talk. Before World War II, no one was sure what Hitler would do next – this is the enigma, or "mystery," of the title.

"If Hitler were to ever conquer Europe, he would do away with hysterics of my kind... Hitler interested me purely as a focus for my own mania and because he struck me as having an unequaled disaster value."

Salvador Dali

Dali in the United States

▲ New York's famous Manhattan skyline in the 1940s seemed to sum up America's glamorous image.

In the mid-1930s, the United States was emerging from the years of depression that had followed the Wall Street Crash of 1929. To many Europeans, the U.S. seemed to be full of energy and hope once again, just as it had been in the start of the 20th century. They were excited by American music, by the dizzying skyscrapers of America's bustling cities, and by Hollywood movies and their glamorous stars. Everything about Europe, by contrast, seemed tired and old-fashioned.

LIVING THE AMERICAN DREAM

During his visits to the United States in the 1930s, Dali had fallen in love with the country. When he and Gala went to live there in 1940, they were already well known and had a wide circle of friends. They lived at the house of a rich American woman named Caresse Crosby in the state of Virginia. Dali was much sought after by high-society hostesses and journalists and had plenty of offers of work.

A SECRET LIFE

American magazines liked to report on Dali's eccentric lifestyle. One report called "Dali's Daffy Day" included a picture of the painter at work, sitting on a chair balanced on four turtles. Dali also attracted attention in 1942, when he published his autobiography *The Secret Life of Salvador Dali*. The book is full of fantastic stories about Dali's early life. Some of the stories are true, while others Dali made-up. He believed that, like fake jewels, false memories were "the most real, the most brilliant."

IN THE MONEY

In the United States, Dali made a lot of money by painting portraits of famous people and designing advertisements. André Breton accused Dali of being greedy, and joked that he was "Avida Dollars," that is, "mad about dollars." (Avida Dollars is an anagram of the name Salvador Dali.)

Dali also went to work in Hollywood. He helped the director Alfred Hitchcock (1889-1980) make his thriller *Spellbound* (1945). In the movie, a psychiatrist solves a murder by analyzing her patient's dreams. Dali designed the film sets used to represent the man's dreams.

▲ *The Moon, Woman Cuts the Circle*, Jackson Pollock, c. 1943. Jackson Pollock was one of a new generation of American artists who were taking art in radical and exciting directions. As a result, New York was replacing Paris as the center of the art world.

▲ A scene designed by Dali for the dream sequences of Hitchcock's *Spellbound*. Alfred Hitchcock was one of the leading film directors of the time, and it says a lot about Dali's status as a popular artist since he was invited to work with him.

THE ATOMIC AGE

In 1941, Germany's ally Japan bombed Pearl Harbor, a U.S. naval base in Hawaii, and the United States entered the war on the side of Britain. The war came to an end in 1945, soon after a U.S. plane dropped the first atomic bomb on Hiroshima, Japan, killing 240,000 people. This terrible explosion filled Dali with wonder rather than horror. He wrote that the explosion of an atomic bomb reminded him of "mossy and mushroomy trees of an earthly paradise."

The Man With the Mustache

▲ Dali in his studio at Port Lligat in the 1950s. A cross hangs on the wall above him.

Dali and Gala did not return to Europe until 1949. For the rest of his life, Dali would be an international star – as famous for his long, curly mustache and walking stick as for his paintings. He loved to appear on television, and he wrote more books full of stories about his life. In 1954, he even published a book about his own mustache!

"I shall use my work to show the unity of the universe, by showing the spirituality of all substance."

Salvador Dali

MYSTICAL EXPERIENCES

Dali was brought up in a strong, Roman Catholic country. Although Dali's father did not believe in a god, his mother was very religious. Nevertheless, until the 1940s, Dali paid little attention to religion in his work, except to occasionally poke fun at it. After World War II, he became drawn to religion and to mysticism. A mystic has religious experiences such as visions that bring him or her into direct contact with God. Dali saw such experiences as Surrealist because they seemed to belong to the world of the imagination and the unconscious mind.

Dali's later work includes many religious paintings. These pictures are very unusual and some people have questioned the sincerity of Dali's belief. Others have found his religious work profoundly moving.

TURNING TO RELIGION

Dali and Gala divided their time between Paris, New York, and Port Lligat, enjoying a life of luxury. This only left Dali time to paint while visiting Port Lligat. After the war, many of his paintings were about religion. In 1955, Dali visited the Pope, and in 1958, he and Gala were married again in a church.

◀ Salvador Dali in front of one of his paintings in 1957. As usual he is holding a walking stick. He also wears a Catalan cap, or *barretina* (see page 9).

TIMELINE ▶

1945	August 1945	1949	1954	1955	1958	1961
Dali works with director Alfred Hitchcock on the film *Spellbound*.	The U.S. drops the first atomic bomb on Hiroshima, Japan.	Dali and Gala return to Europe.	*Dali's Mustache* is published.	Dali meets the Pope.	Dali marries Gala in church.	The Soviet Union puts the first human into space.

Christ of St. John of the Cross, 1951

oil on canvas, 81 x 45 $^2/_3$ in (205 x 116 cm), St. Mungo Museum of Religious Art and Life, Glasgow, Scotland

The inspiration for this painting came from the vision of a 16th-century preacher called Saint John of the Cross. In the vision, the preacher saw Christ from above, as if from heaven. In Dali's painting of the vision, the viewer seems to be floating in the air, gazing down on the cross from a dizzying height.

The Final Performance

THE THEATER-MUSEUM

In 1960, the mayor of Figueres asked Dali to donate one of his paintings to the town museum. Dali refused. Instead, he promised to build a whole museum! The Theater-Museum opened in 1974, when Dali was 70 years old.

From outside the museum looks very different from most art museums. The walls are bright pink, and rows of huge golden eggs line the roof. The interior of the museum is just as strange. For example, in one room, there is a bed with fish for its feet. Standing next to the bed is the skeleton of a gorilla, painted gold.

▲ Dali holds up a picture of Gala. This photograph was taken after her death in 1982. Dali never recovered from the loss of his beloved wife.

Even as he grew older, Dali continued to be interested in the world around him. He was fascinated by developments in physics and genetics and incorporated these interests into his art. He began to paint using an optical instrument called a Wheatstone stereoscope (right). Stereoscopy is the science of how the human eye sees in three dimensions rather than just two. Dali thought of the gift of sight as something spiritual and almost miraculous.

▲ Outside of the Theater-Museum, Figueres. The building itself is a great Surrealist work of art.

LAST YEARS OF GRIEF

Dali carried on a life in the media spotlight. In 1964, he published a second autobiography, which he half-jokingly, half-boastfully called *My Life as a Genius*. In 1982, Gala died and Dali was so grief-stricken that he, too, became ill. Thereafter he lived his life in virtual seclusion, cared for by nurses. He died in 1989, and was buried beneath the Theater-Museum in Figueres.

TIMELINE ▶

1964	1974	1975	1982	June 1982	July 1982	1983	1989
Dali's second autobiography, *My Life as a Genius*, is published.	The Theater-Museum opens in Figueres.	Franco dies. Spain becomes a democratic country headed by a monarch.	The Salvador Dali Museum opens in St. Petersburg, Florida.	Gala dies.	The Spanish king, Juan Carlos, gives Dali the title of Marquis of Púbol.	Dali finishes his last painting, *The Swallow's Tail*.	Dali dies at Figueres on January 23rd.

Dali From the Back Painting Gala From the Back Externalized by Six Virtual Corneas Provisionally Reflected in Six Real Mirrors (unfinished), 1972–73

oil on canvas, (one section of two), 23 2/3 x 23 2/3 in (60 x 60 cm), Gala-Salvador Dali Foundation, Figueres, Spain

Dali's later paintings are sometimes very complicated. In this work, he used a stereoscope to give the viewer the sensation of looking into a real space and not just onto a flat canvas. Here there are multiple layers of "real" space – from the painting itself to the mirror and the landscape outside the window. We are looking at Dali painting Gala watching Dali, who looks back at her – and us – out of the mirror!

"The most extraordinary being you could possibly encounter, the superstar..."

Salvador Dali on Gala

Dali's Legacy

Salvador Dali is one of the most popular modern painters. His paintings and objects are still able to surprise and shock us, or even make us laugh. Although many of the themes that Dali painted in his art are very serious, he always wanted his paintings to entertain the people looking at them. Because of this, some critics think of Dali as a kind of showman or as a magician performing tricks.

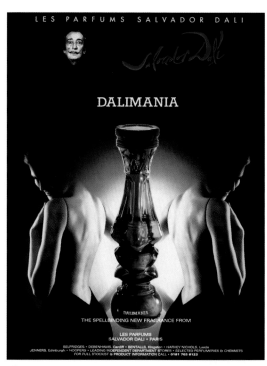

▲ Dali enjoyed being famous and was happy to make money from of his fame. This perfume bearing his name was launched in 1983.

REACT TO THE IMAGE

Many people find modern artists difficult to understand. Dali tried to appeal to people in a simple and direct way. In fact, he didn't want people to understand his paintings at all, but to react to them just as if they were their own dreams. Everyone would shiver if they saw a swarm of ants on their hand. Everyone is puzzled and disturbed when they see something that is normally solid melting, such as the watches on the beach.

▲ Dali's popular appeal has meant Surrealist images have entered our everyday life, through television and advertising.

"The secret of my influence has always been that it remained secret."

Salvador Dali

POP ART

Dali's directness, sense of fun, and popular appeal are his most important legacies to modern art. Many artists working today want to make art not just for a small band of experts but for a wide audience made up of all sorts of people. This was one of the aims of the Pop artists who worked during the 1960s and early 1970s. The most famous Pop artist is Andy Warhol (1928-87). Warhol used popular images from newspapers, film, TV, and even everyday products such as soup cans to create entertaining artworks.

▲ Like Dali, Damien Hirst has become famous for shocking us.

ARTIST AS SHOWMAN

Damien Hirst (b.1966) is a modern British artist who has learned a great deal from Dali. Hirst is not really a painter or a sculptor. Like Dali, he is a showman, a conjurer of surprising and shocking objects. Some of his most famous works have consisted of dead animals such as cows and sharks sliced in half and displayed in cases. Naturally enough, we are revolted and upset by such sights. However, Hirst's artwork, like Dali's, can also lead us to ponder serious subjects such as death and decay. These are the very same subjects artists have been dealing with for hundreds of years.

◄ Pop artist Andy Warhol developed Dali's ideas about how ordinary, everyday objects could be made extraordinary. Warhol, like Dali, also became famous for his appearance.

Two Catalan Surrealists

Dali was not the only Surrealist painter from Catalonia. Joan Miró (1893-1983) came from there, too. To begin with, the two artists were friendly and admired each other's paintings. Slightly older than Dali, Miró encouraged the young artist to broaden his horizons. In Paris in 1929, Miró introduced Dali to the Surrealists. Over the years, the two artists' work developed in very different directions (see Miró's work on pages 18 and 24).

> *You are without doubt a very gifted man with a brilliant career ahead of you – in Paris!*

▲ **After visiting Dali's studio in Figueres in 1927, Miró wrote to him, encouraging him to come to Paris to further his career.**

> *Miró returns the line, dot, ... and colors to their pure, elemental, magical possibilities... Miró's art is too big for the stupid world of our artists and intellectuals.*

◀ **Dali was also enthusiastic about Miró's work. He wrote this in a review of an exhibition of Miró's paintings in 1928.**

JOAN MIRÓ

Joan Miró grew up on a farm near Barcelona and was very proud of being Catalan. His paintings often include Catalan symbols such as the *barettina*. Even after he moved to Paris in 1919, he always spent the summers on his father's farm.

Miró was one of the first artists to join the Surrealist group. He signed the first *Surrealist Manifesto*, and remained committed to the group's ideals. Like the other Surrealists, Miró used his art to explore the unconscious mind. During his early career, he lived in great poverty and was near starvation. He even wrote that one of his paintings was inspired "by my hallucinations brought on by hunger." Miró loved music and poetry and tried to capture their qualities in his art.

▶ **Miró working on a painting, 1967.**

TIMELINE ▶

1904	1921	1924	1928	1930
May 11, 1904 Salvador Dali Domènech is born in Figueres, Catalonia, Spain.	**October 1921** Goes to the San Fernando Academy of Fine Art, Madrid.	**May 1924** Serves a one-month prison sentence.	**March 1928** Publishes the *Yellow Manifesto*.	**January 1930** De Rivera dictatorship ends.
1908 Sister, Ana Mariá, is born.	**1922** The Surrealist group forms in Paris.	**October 1924** *Surrealist Manifesto* published.	**April 1929** Makes movie *Un chien andalou* with Buñuel.	**April 1930** Designs frontispiece of *The Second Surrealist Manifesto*.
1914 Gaudí's Güell Park opens in Barcelona.	**1923** Freud's *The Interpretation of Dreams* is published in Spanish.	**November 1925** First solo exhibition held in Barcelona.	**Summer 1929** Begins affair with Gala Éluard.	**Summer 1930** Buys home Port Lligat, Cadaqués.
1914-1918 World War I.	**September 1923** De Rivero dictator of Spain.	**April 1926** First trip to Paris; visits Picasso and Miró.	**October 1929** *Un chien andalou* opens in Paris. The Wall Street Crash.	**October 1930** *L'Âge d'or*, a new Dali-Buñuel film, opens in Paris.
1917 Holds an exhibition in the family apartment.	**October 1923** Suspended by the Academy.	**October 1926** Expelled from the Academy.	**November 1929** Has his first exhibition in Paris.	**December 1930** *The Visible Woman* is published.
February 1921 Dali's mother dies.		**January 1927** Dali has his second one-man show.		

CONTRASTING PERSONALITIES

The two artists' personalities were very different. Miró was very modest and disliked appearing in public. He thought that Dali was too eager to be famous. When Dali began to design clothes, Miró accused him of being a "painter of neckties." The two men also had opposing political views. During the Spanish Civil War, Miró supported the Republicans, whereas Dali refused to take sides (see page 25).

The spectacle of the sky overwhelms me. I'm overwhelmed when I see, in an immense sky, the crescent of the moon, or the sun. It is there, in my pictures: tiny forms in huge empty spaces. Empty spaces, empty horizons, empty plains …

▲ **Miró points to the inspiration behind his art.**

▶ **Dali was always much more arrogant than Miró. He seemed to find inspiration in himself. He loved being famous.** ▼

The only difference between me and the Surrealists is that I am a Surrealist.

Every morning when I awake the greatest of joys is mine – that of being Salvador Dali.

Miró was the very incarnation of freedom. His art was airier, freer, lighter than anything I had seen before.

◀ **Dali and Miró attracted very different admirers. The Swiss Surrealist sculptor Alberto Giacometti (1901-66) was a close friend of Miró and wrote this about his art.**

▶ **U.S. artist Andy Warhol got to know Dali and Gala in the 1960s. Warhol did not seem interested in Dali's art. He liked Dali because he was a star.**

It's like being with royalty or circus people. That's why I like being with Dali – because it's not like being with an artist…

1931	1934	1938	1942	1964
1931 Spain is declared a republic.	**November 1934** Visits New York for the first time.	**March 1938** Hitler makes Austria part of Germany.	**October 1942** *The Secret Life of Salvador Dali* is published.	**1964** *My Life as a Genius* is published.
January 1933 Adolf Hitler gains power in Germany.	**June 1936** Attends International Surrealist Exhibition in London.	**July 1938** Meets Freud.	**1945** Works on the film *Spellbound*.	**1974** The Theater-Museum opens in Figueres.
November 1933 First solo exhibition in the U.S.	**1936-39** The Spanish Civil War.	**Early 1939** Expelled from Surrealist group.	**1949** Returns to Europe.	**1975** Franco dies. Spain becomes a democracy.
January 1934 Marries Gala.	**December 1936** On the front cover of *Time*.	**1939-45** World War II.	**1954** *Dali's Mustache* is published.	**June 1982** Gala dies.
1934 Moving away from the Surrealist group.	**January 1938** Takes part in International Surrealists Exhibition in Paris.	**August 1940** Goes to the United States.	**1955** Meets the Pope.	**1983** Finishes last painting, *The Swallow's Tail*.
Ocotober 1934 First solo exhibition in Britain.		**November 1941** Has joint exhibition with Miró at the Museum of Modern Art, New York.	**1958** Marries Gala in church.	**1989** Dali dies at Figueres on January 23.

Glossary

anarchism: the belief that people should be able to live their lives free of church or government laws.

avant-garde: describes new, experimental, or radical ideas.

collage: a picture made by pasting photographs, newspaper cuttings, string, labels, and other objects on to a flat surface.

communism: a political system first suggested by Karl Marx (1818-83) under which every one shares a country's goods and property.

Cubism: the name of an art movement evolving in Paris around 1907 led by Pablo Picasso (1881-1973) and Georges Braque (1882-1963). The Cubists painted multiple angles of a person or object so they were all seen at once.

dictator: a ruler who has total control over a country.

empire: a large number of countries ruled by a more powerful country.

enigma: a mystery.

Expressionism: an approach to painting which communicates an emotional state of mind rather than external reality. The Norwegian artist Edvard Munch (1863-1944), who painted *The Scream*, was a leading Expressionist.

fascist: describes an extreme right-wing political system where government has total power, usually focused around a charismatic leader.

frottage: using rubbings of a surface to obtain a textured effect.

genetics: the study of genes, the parts of living cells that are duplicated from one generation to the next and determine heredity.

hallucination: something which the mind sees or experiences but does not exist in reality.

Impressionists: a group of artists based in Paris during the late nineteenth century who painted "impressions" of the world with broad brushstrokes of pure, unmixed color. The group included Auguste Renoir (1841-1919), Claude Monet (1840-1926), and Edgar Degas (1834-1917).

left-wing: a word used to describe socialist or communist political views.

manifesto: a declaration of beliefs.

monarchy: a system of government headed by a king or queen.

montage: a method of editing film so that the picture cuts quickly from one image to another.

mysticism: a devout form of religious belief where a person has direct contact with God through spiritual experiences such as visions.

Nazi: anything to do with the National Socialist German Workers' Party, the extreme right-wing political party led by Adolf Hitler that ruled Germany between 1933 and 1945.

Old Masters: the name used to describe the greatest European painters from around 1500-1800, including Leonardo da Vinci (1452-1519), Michelangelo (1475-1564), Velázquez (1599-1660), and Jan Vermeer (1632-75).

Pop art: the art movement that emerged in the United States in the 1960s which tried to make art more popular by featuring everyday objects, famous people, or well-known designs. Andy Warhol (1928-87) was one of the most famous Pop artists.

republic: a system of government headed by an elected president.

right-wing: adjective used to describe conservative or traditionalist political views.

Roman Catholicism: one of the major Christian churches; the leader of the Roman Catholic Church is the Pope, who lives in the Vatican City in Rome.

socialism: a political system in which the government tries to make sure that everyone has a fair income and equal rights.

Surrealism: an intellectual movement that emerged in the 1920s that tried to depict the life of our unconscious minds and dreams. The Surrealists included artists, writers, and filmmakers.

unconscious: describes the part of a person's mind that lies outside the conscious mind we use in everyday waking life. Dreams and the imagination are expressions of the unconscious.

Museums and Galleries

Works by Dali are exhibited in museums and galleries all around the world. Some of the ones listed here are devoted solely to Dali, but most have a wide range of other artists' works on display.

Even if you can't visit any of these galleries yourself, you may be able to visit their web sites. Gallery web sites often show pictures of the artworks they have on display. Some of the web sites even offer virtual tours which allow you to wander around and look at different paintings while sitting comfortably in front of your computer. Most of the international web sites listed below include an option that allows you to view them in English.

Dali Universe, London
County Hall
Riverside Building
London SE1 7PB
www.daliuniverse.com

Fundació Gala-Salvador Dali
This organization runs three Dali museums in Spain (listed below). Their web site connects to all three museums.
www.dali-estate.org

Dali Theater-Museum
Plaça Gala i Salvador Dali, s/s
17600 Figueres
Spain

Gala-Dali Castle Museum-House, Spain
Casa-Museu Castell Gala Dali
Púbol
17120 la Pera
Spain

Salvador Dali Museum-House
Port Lligat
Cadaqués
Spain

Salvador Dali Art Gallery
A virtual art gallery featuring 1,500 of Dali's works.
www.dali-gallery.com

Salvador Dali Museum, St. Petersburg
1000 Third Street South
St. Petersburg, FL 33701-4901
www.salvadordalimuseum.org

Museum of Modern Art, New York
(Under renovation until 2005.
See web site for further details.)
11 West 53 Street
New York, NY 10019
www.moma.org

Museo Nacional Centro de Arte Reina Sofia
Santa Isabel, 52
Madrid
Spain
http://museoreinasofia.mcu.es

National Gallery of Australia
Parkes Place
Canberra
ACT 2601
Australia
www.nga.gov.au

Tate Modern, London
Bankside
London SE1 9TG
www.tate.org.uk

Index